SHADOW AND LIGHT

ORACLE

SHADOW AND LIGHT ORACLE

SELENA MOON

REFLECTION CARDS TO UNLOCK YOUR UNCONSCIOUS MIND

ROCKPOOL

A Rockpool book
PO Box 252
Summer Hill
NSW 2130
Australia

rockpoolpublishing.com

Follow us! **f** ⓘ rockpoolpublishing
Tag your images with #rockpoolpublishing

ISBN: 9781922579638

Published in 2023 by Rockpool Publishing
Copyright text and images © Selena Moon, 2023
Copyright design © Rockpool Publishing, 2023

Design and typesetting by Daniel Poole, Rockpool Publishing
Edited by Brooke Halliwell

Printed and bound in China
10 9 8 7 6 5 4 3 2 1

Contents

Introduction

✦

Say welcome to your new best friend! *Shadow & Light Oracle* is designed to support you on your journey of personal growth, self-improvement, confidence and overall well-being.

We all go through different phases, pains and struggles and life constantly throws us curveballs. Sometimes it gets overwhelming and we find it difficult to talk about certain topics; that's where this deck can help. Like a friend you confide in or who supports you through the hard times, and in good times it offers you a little bit of reflection or a push to inspire you to move forward and keep working on yourself and your goals in life.

Shadow & Light Oracle is perfect to use when you feel stuck and don't know in which direction to go, or when you are overthinking (who doesn't?) and need a new angle to get your thinking pattern out of the repetitive loop. These cards offer you a mirror into your thoughts with multiple angles to view them. They are designed to give new insight into your own mind and help you to reflect on your thoughts, behaviour and feelings.

Each card represents reflecting or opposing ideas of different aspects in life. They touch on a multitude of topics that we all go through at some point. There are a total of 36 cards with each card offering two perspectives totalling in 72 overall themes. One thing can always be looked at from at least two perspectives and this is what these cards aim to highlight – there can be two sides of one story or two components of the same story.

This is a very intimate deck for me as all messages are derived from personal experiences and insights I have learned on my own path of self-growth. It is written from my point of view and shouldn't necessarily be read as hard facts, but rather different perspectives to reflect upon. These are all ideas and views I wish I had learned earlier, but it's never too late to improve and I will keep working on myself and I hope this deck inspires you to do the same!

How to use the cards

✦

CLEANSING YOUR DECK

Before using the deck I suggest you cleanse it to help you connect with it and bring your focus in on the reading. Below are some suggestions for cleansing.

- ✦ Burn some sage and flow the deck through the smoke.

- ✦ Hold the deck in your hands, close your eyes and when you inhale imagine a bright light going into the deck and when you exhale a dark cloud of smoke going out from the deck.

- ✦ Place a clear quartz crystal on top of your deck and leave it overnight.

THE CARDS

This deck has specifically been created for readings on yourself. It is very personal and touches on many sensitive topics. Use the cards whenever you feel like there is something you need to get off your chest or need clarity with, anything you feel stuck on or if you just want to sit with yourself and see what comes up for you right now.

Each card has a description but I encourage you to read the imagery intuitively and create your own meaning from what you see. Start with your first impression and then read the descriptions to get further insight.

Each description will also give you an affirmation; use this at any time to remind yourself of the message from that card.

It also gives you a practical exercise that you can do to help you move through the issues you might have with the topic on that specific card.

There is no wrong way of using the deck; whatever feels right for you is the way to move forward with it.

QUESTIONS TO ASK

Sometimes it can be tricky to come up with clear questions to get the most out of your reading. Open-ended questions can give you more insight than a standard yes or no question which may be difficult to interpret. For example, if you are struggling to choose between two options you could ask the card to show you the outcome for the two different paths which may help to guide you in the right direction.

Other questions you could use if it suits your situation: How will choosing option A benefit me? What are the obstacles I might face if I choose this option? What do I need to know before moving ahead?

In general, questions beginning with how and what tend to give more meaningful answers rather than will it and when.

It's a good idea to sit and reflect for a while before you ask what it is that you really want to know. It might take some time to formulate your question and that is okay. You can write down a few options and see if it will help you come closer to what you really want to gain insight on.

If any answers you get don't make sense, always go back to your original question and see if it needs to be refined to get a clearer picture from the cards.

If you are unsure what to ask or just want to get straight into your reading you can use the suggested card spreads to get started quickly.

Card spreads

ONE-CARD SPREAD

This simple spread can be used in many different ways.

You can pull one card every day and reflect on it. What event today is represented in this card? This is a good way of connecting with and getting to know your deck.

You can ask a simple question of any kind and pull a card to see what answer you get. Or pull one card without any intention set to see what message the deck gives you; this is likely something you need to hear right now.

REFLECTION SPREAD

Reflecting is all about looking at the same thing from different perspectives. This spread is great to use when you are feeling stuck or lost in your thought patterns. It can help you view things differently. Focus on a specific problem you'd like to get a resolution for or think differently about. Write it down or keep it at the forefront of your mind when pulling the cards.

- **Card 1:** the problem
- **Card 2:** another way to look at the problem
- **Card 3:** a solution to the problem
- **Card 4:** another possible solution to the
  same problem

SELF-REFLECTION SPREAD

Reflecting on yourself is always helpful for your personal growth. Use this spread at any time to get some new insights!

- ◆ **Card 1:** my current situation or feeling
- ◆ **Card 2:** my fears around the situation
- ◆ **Card 3:** my wishes and wants around the situation
- ◆ **Card 4:** my insecurities around the situation
- ◆ **Card 5:** a solution to overcoming my fears
- ◆ **Card 6:** a way to achieve my wishes and wants
- ◆ **Card 7:** a solution to handling my insecurities

ORACLE CARDS

Growth • Pain

Growth ✦ Pain

There can be no growth without pain. We often resist change and growth because it might be painful to let go of what is known to us. We fear what we could become without it. It is easy to fall into the habit of focusing too much on what we leave behind rather than what we have to gain.

You may feel stuck where you're at and fail to realise that you are on a constant journey of growth. Your actions, experiences and previous thoughts and emotions are your roots and they will always be a part of you, but on the other hand you can use these to your advantage and grow new branches that you have never thought of before. While things are taking form it might feel turbulent and painful but eventually these things will become part of your stable roots.

Ask yourself how you think about change and growth, what are the things you are resisting, and what are the things you have to gain?

The pain we experience when going through growth may have originated from the fear of showing our true selves, our insecurities and vulnerability. To truly grow, acknowledge that it is okay not to be perfect, find courage to face your own fears and the strength to tear down or lower your wall of judgement towards yourself and others.

AFFIRMATION: 'I embrace the pain and make way for growth.'

EXERCISE: Make a list of all the things you will gain from letting go of your fears. Read the list out loud to yourself twice each day either in the morning or before you go to bed or take time and meditate upon your list.

Discomfort ✦ Resentment

We often avoid conflicts or even mentioning our feelings because we fear the discomfort it might cause especially in relationships and even more so in new relationships. It's common to avoid conflicts by focusing solely on the positive things and ignoring negative emotions that need to be addressed just to keep the peace between everyone involved. Direct communication isn't always something that comes easy though, it needs to be learned, and this is an indication for you to practise it. Not communicating directly can instead cause the thing we fear from communication.

If you keep repressing your emotions by not speaking up or not allowing your concerns to be aired these can grow into resentment towards your partner in unhealthy proportions. By avoiding discomfort or conflict, instead of building love and trust, we build resentment towards the people we love. That feeling of resentment can become worse than discomfort, since resentment keeps growing until the matter is resolved.

Sometimes it's better to endure the uncomfortable to avoid living with two selves: one loving and one resenting. Eventually it only becomes your own pain that nobody else can see. You don't need to hide yourself to keep the peace. Stand up and face your fear and you might get to experience the calm behind the storm.

Take the time to reflect upon what is bothering you in your relationships and what you have been letting slide. What issues have you been feeling hesitant to bring up? When you have gathered your thoughts, be brave and choose discomfort over resentment.

This card is an encouragement to you if you are feeling resentful towards someone, to try and bring to the surface what has been bothering you.

AFFIRMATION: 'I choose discomfort over resentment.'

EXERCISE: Learn to recognise the feeling of resentment by paying attention to your daily interactions with the people you are close to. Whenever the feeling arises make a mental note that you are feeling resentful. This way you can learn what things you need to speak up about next time.

Generosity ✦ Egoism

Are you truly giving without expecting anything in return? A lot of transactions we make, whether it be with acquaintances or loved ones, often have a hidden agenda rather than just giving for the sake of giving. It might be to show someone how thoughtful we are, to receive something in return or to make ourselves look superior.

Thoughts like 'why isn't anybody thinking about me?' or 'I wish someone would show me how special I am to them' might have crossed your mind but have you tried to reverse the thought and give to others what you are seeking? We are often so caught up in our own minds and what we want that we forget to give with our heart to the people we are closest to what we secretly expect or wish from them.

Do you know someone who seems to give to you only to expect something in return or show that they could afford more than you? Their heart might not be true. Keep a lookout for these people in your surroundings and you might start to notice who are really caring and who have a hidden agenda.

Generosity is about letting go of the ego and giving with your whole heart to show that you truly care and want someone else to feel good.

AFFIRMATION: 'I give with a true heart.'

EXERCISE: Think about a friend or loved one that you haven't really appreciated lately. Think about something you could do for them or give them that would make them truly happy. Maybe send a surprise gift or just a special e-card. It doesn't have to be anything fancy or expensive, just think about something special that you don't give on a daily basis. Even if it's just a random message to tell them you love them.

4

Reflection • Overthinking

Reflection ✦ Overthinking

Overthinking is extremely common and something most of us do. Things such as asking yourself 'what if?' repeatedly; picturing worst-case scenarios or exaggerating the severity of an issue; constantly looking in the mirror and analysing things about ourselves that aren't necessarily true. And the more you do it, the truer they feel to you. So, it's worth taking a step back and starting to think about the things you are telling yourself, what you see might not be what others see.

Your thoughts can both aggravate you, cause frustration, anger and sadness, but they can also bring you peace and harmony and a way of coping with complicated emotions. Practice changing or steering the direction your thoughts are taking regarding an issue and rather than worry, reflect without judgement.

The first step is to start noticing when your thoughts are causing pain and you feel like everything is burning. Make a note to yourself every time you feel heated. Only once you start to realise when it's happening will you be able to stop yourself and bring that fiery feeling back to a more peaceful place in your mind.

Reflect by observing and acknowledging your own thoughts and start communicating with them in a more objective way. Start to oppose the 'truths' you are telling yourself. Are they really true? Do you have evidence? Might there be alternative ways to think about the same problem?

AFFIRMATION: 'I have power over my thoughts.'

EXERCISE: Get a nice piece of paper, perhaps in your favourite colour, and write down these three questions:

22

1. Do I have proof?

2. What might be an alternative truth?

3. What soothing thing can I tell myself?

Put it in a frame and hang it somewhere you can see it, perhaps near your bed where a lot of overthinking might be happening so that every time you start worrying, you can look at these questions and start answering them to calm your mind.

Self-doubt ✦ Hope

As newborns, self-doubt is not a concept that is yet developed. Even in young children, the thought that they won't be able to do something doesn't occur as much. For example, when a child starts walking they will keep falling over, but the child doesn't for a second think that walking is not for them, they can't do it and won't keep trying, they will get up again and again until they are able to stand up, walk and even run. The child keeps trying until they succeed. This confidence, the notion of never giving up, slowly gets lost over time in a society that constantly compares achievements and everyone's successes are on display. It's easy to feel inadequate.

If you've pulled this card, it's an indication that you need to find courage to believe in yourself again, dig a bit deeper and see if you can find that spirit you used to have as a baby that failing is not an option, it's only a matter of how many times you have to try.

If you are doubting yourself about something, be brave and give yourself a chance to succeed. There is a path forward for you, you just need to go with the flow that you're feeling inside. If you never try something because you are doubting yourself, there is a 100 per cent chance you won't succeed. Hang on to that hope that you have, hope that whatever it is you are having doubts about, can and will be something good.

Even if you try and don't succeed, you have already won because you gave yourself a chance and next time it will be easier to do the same again. Eventually that hope will show itself worthy.

AFFIRMATION: 'I will give myself a chance to succeed.'

EXERCISE: Imagine something you've wanted for a long time but never dared to try and go for. Write it down on a piece of paper or in your journal.

Underneath, make a list of small steps you could take to get closer to achieving this or things that could help you along the way to make the journey a little easier or make you feel more comfortable in taking the first step. Then start taking those small steps, one by one.

Shadow ✦ Light

Life is a constant roller coaster; nothing is permanent and circumstances change all the time. There cannot be any concept of light if darkness does not exist and there couldn't be any shadows without the light. If the light was constant, we wouldn't appreciate it and we appreciate the dark only because we've experienced the light.

This also relates to similar emotional concepts, not only literally. We all have light and darkness within us, light and happy thoughts, dark and depressing thoughts, light sides of ourselves that we'd love to show to other people, but also darker sides we prefer to keep to ourselves.

Light, happy, positive feelings are easy to deal with, almost so easy that they can sometimes pass barely being acknowledged. Dark, sad and negative thoughts and feelings can be harder to handle. Those dark thoughts might get acknowledged and result in suffering or they might get ignored and pushed away to become less apparent in your life; however, pushing those feelings away and not dealing with them might cloud your happiness in the long term.

This card encourages you to think about how you handle light and darkness in your life. Do you take the time to celebrate the bright moments enough and recognise what you have to be grateful for? And equally, how do you handle the darkness? Is it being recognised for what it is, do you work through it or are you trying to push it away?

If you truly want to enjoy your brightest moments, be brave enough to explore what's in the shadows so you can blow away any upcoming dark clouds and enjoy the light again.

AFFIRMATION: 'I see you, pain; I feel you, pain; I give you permission to move through.'

EXERCISE: The first step to moving through difficult emotions is to acknowledge them. Practice taking this first step whenever you realise there is some darkness that needs to be dealt with.

Use any of the mantras 'I notice that I feel …' (or come up with your own that works for you). Fill in the dots with whatever feeling you have noticed. If you don't know exactly what you feel you can voice that too and just acknowledge that you feel *something* that is uncomfortable.

You can either voice this in your head or write it down if it feels more helpful.

Love ✦ Hurt

There is seldom love without hurt and we must be willing to risk feeling hurt in order to gain the ultimate and exquisite feeling of love – both for others and by others.

If you've ever experienced that unreal feeling you might feel convinced it's worth the pain that comes with it; however, if you've experienced awful feelings of hurt you might have opposite feelings towards it. You might feel that it's not worth it at all. But the longer time goes without daring to love and be loved again, the more you are missing out on.

It's easy to think that love is the reward we get for putting up with the hurt. But what if we could turn around that perspective? What if we could see the hurt as a lesson and look at it from the outside and think 'What has this hurt taught me about love?' Instead of feeling that we have to sacrifice something for love, we can collect little messages to use to grow the love instead.

Passively waiting for the pain to pass or for the love to flourish is not going to be enough. It might only overwhelm you with negative feelings and dreams that might never come true. Love is not a thing that happens, it is something that you do, therefore, it needs to be worked on. By dealing with the pain and going through it you give love a chance to flourish around you.

AFFIRMATION: 'I accept the hurt that comes with love as a lesson to help me move forward.'

EXERCISE: Use your most hurtful love experience as an example. Write down the things that happened that made you feel hurt. Next to each point, write down what this has taught you.

This might not be easy or obvious straight away but you can keep working on the list and keep it in your mind until you have worked out what the lesson was.

Use this list to help you navigate towards better relationships and hopefully less hurt.

Relationship ✦ Solitude

Relationships and solitude work in symbiosis; strive to keep a healthy balance at a level that works for you. It might not be the same for everyone, some people require more alone time and some don't need as much. Have a think, which type do you think you are? Are you currently achieving your ideal balance?

Dissatisfaction with either solitude or partnership might be caused by the lack of the other. Unhappiness in a relationship may result from not enough solitude or not feeling good in your solitude. Feeling lonely, on the other hand, can be caused by an unsatisfactory relationship.

In romantic relationships it can be hard to create a balance between these two; there can easily be too much of one of them and not enough of the other. Even if you might have balance in terms of the amount between the two, the quality also counts. Maybe you are getting a lot of alone time, but you don't value it as much because you find it hard to enjoy it. If this is the case, take a moment to think about how you can embrace your alone time more. Can you do something that will fill up your heart as much as being together with someone does?

This card encourages you to take a closer look at both your relationships and your solitude. Are you living in a bubble with your significant other or are you starting to become a unit with no separate lives? Do you feel like your partner is always too far away, never spending enough time with you, going on their own adventures? Or it might be you that is always looking outside the relationship and finding your own happiness without including them.

Think about if there is something you can do to make your relationship more meaningful together if that's what you need right now, or is there something you can do that makes your solitude more rewarding so you have more to give in your relationships?

AFFIRMATION: 'I welcome my alone time as much as my relationships.'

EXERCISE: Regardless of whether you are in a relationship or not, spend some time figuring out what things you like to do when you are not in a relationship and what things you enjoy doing with your significant other. Write them down on separate notes and put them in two separate bowls.

If you are in a relationship, compare the activities that you currently do. Are they equal? Do you spend your time mainly in your solitude activity bowl or in the relationship activity bowl?

If you are single, when you are feeling bored you can revisit your solitude activity bowl and get tips from yourself on how to feel more joyful. And if you happen to enter a relationship you can use the bowls to remind yourself to keep doing the things you enjoy and at the same time enjoy the things from the relationship activity bowl.

Vulnerability · Empathy

Empathy is the ability to truly feel and be with someone in their feelings. To walk together with them on a dark road. It is not standing beside and waving at them but truly being there for them. To hold their hand and drown with them for a moment and be able to feel their emotions. By understanding how they feel you can help to pull them up to the surface again. To be able to say 'I feel sorry with you' instead of 'I feel sorry for you'. Let their feelings blossom in their darkness, let them spread out and in that way they can be freed of some of the pain.

When we are vulnerable, we let other people in. It is the way we can show them the dark path we are taking with all its flaws and nastiness. We let them see the parts of us we have tried to hide deep under the surface, therefore empathy cannot exist without vulnerability. If you don't dare to show yourself and what you truly feel, it is almost impossible for others to understand you and show empathy towards you.

This card challenges you to think of your vulnerability as an asset rather than a liability. As a strength rather than a weakness. A true power within you. You have so much to gain from showing your true self.

It might feel extremely scary to show your vulnerability in front of someone, but don't you admire people that do this? Don't you think of them as brave and strong? Showing vulnerability is often seen as being weak, but it's actually being extremely strong. Someone opening up to you might make it easier for you to open up to them and likewise you can help someone else to release their feelings by revealing yours to them. A bond of trust and empathy can then start to flourish and grow.

AFFIRMATION: 'My vulnerability is my strength.'

EXERCISE: Next time a close friend asks you how you are doing, try and stop for a second and not automatically reply that you're fine if you are not. See if you can be a little more authentic in your response. Start small by admitting it's not the best right now but you are working on it. Or if you are, in fact, extremely happy, try and tell them why – instead of saying great, explain the feelings you have, perhaps it's gratitude or love?

Passion ✦ Purpose

Passion and purpose are deeply connected. Your purpose is what drives you forward, your motivation, your fuel to your engine. But if you are being asked, 'What is your purpose in life?' you might find that a bit difficult to answer straight away. It is something we rarely reflect over; we just do it.

If you were instead asked 'What are you passionate about?' this is more likely to light up a fire inside of you and you know the answer straight away.

By identifying your passion, you will most likely find the answer to what your purpose is somewhere behind it. Look within and see what you can find. Place a hand on your heart and ask yourself what truly makes you happy. In what scenario does time fly and what makes you forget about all the stress you might have?

We often go about our lives without reflecting too much on what we are doing and more importantly why we are doing it. This card is an indication for you to search within yourself, to single out what you are passionate about, what drives you forward and what motivates you to do different things. It's an indication for you to revert to your purpose by focusing on what you love and care about most.

Try and connect with your inner passion and then see how you can use this in your life to create meaning for others, and in return it will help you to feel what your true purpose is. Without sharing your passion and skills with others, it is only a joy and a passion, but by giving to the world you create a purpose.

AFFIRMATION: 'I trust my passion to lead me to my purpose.'

EXERCISE: Simple meditation to find your purpose

Bring your diary or any piece of paper and a pen to write down your thoughts afterwards.

Start your meditation by taking a comfortable seat or you can lie down if that feels more comfortable for you.

Place a hand on your heart and take 3–5 deep breaths to come into the present moment and connect with yourself.

Now, ask yourself what you are passionate about.

Multiple things may come up but focus on the first two or three that come to mind.

Try and really feel them and ask more questions about the details and what part of it makes your heart sing.

Stay in this search for a few minutes or as long as it feels interesting then open your eyes and note down the main passions you identified within yourself.

You have now started this journey in your mind and it can help you to stay focused and connected to your purpose.

Advise · Listen

Advise ✦ Listen

When someone is experiencing hardships, we often like to offer our support in the form of coming up with solutions for them; however, this rarely makes them feel any better and likewise if you're having some issues and people try to suggest solutions you might feel more agitated. Know the feeling?

It's because deep down inside, you have already thought about the different solutions, you already know what action you will eventually take but right now you just want to let the painful emotions flow out of you to relieve the pressure and release the pain.

For the pain to go away, you want to feel heard, you want people to understand what you are feeling and you need your feelings to be validated in this vulnerable situation. It is the same for other people too – they might not want to hear your advice right now; they might just want you to listen.

This card encourages you to stop and think before you offer a solution to anybody or when you are being offered solutions. When it comes to helping others, think about what they are saying and listen carefully before replying. Did they ask for advice? Did they ask you to offer any suggestions on how to resolve their issue or did they perhaps not ask anything at all? If they didn't ask, it's highly likely that what they need is empathy.

If it makes you frustrated when other people are trying to help you through giving advice, think about what it is you would like from them and try to express this beforehand so they know how they can best help you.

AFFIRMATION: 'Deep within, I know how to solve my own problems.'

EXERCISE: Next time you seek support from a friend, practice telling them before you start what you would like to hear from them. For example, say 'I need to tell you about this problem, would you please just listen and validate what I am feeling?'

And next time someone comes to you for comfort, ask them first if they want advice or for you to only listen.

Planning ✦ Destiny

If planning and destiny were sitting on each side of your scale, which one would weigh over? Are you comfortable with that? Some people believe that everything is destiny and nothing ever turns out a way that it shouldn't, and if we think it does, it was for a reason or a purpose.

Sometimes, no matter how much we plan or wish for something, it doesn't come true. Or it comes true in a different way than we expected.

You are planning with your feelings, thinking about what you would like to happen, what you would like to achieve. But sometimes life has a different plan for you and your own plans might be swept away in an instant. It might feel painful and turbulent in the moment, but you will come to realise later that it could have saved you from making a mistake. It may not be obvious at first and you will never see it if you keep looking away and focusing on what you missed out on.

This card suggests that you need to take a closer look at things that have happened in the past that you are unhappy with and see if you can find a reason or purpose behind it turning out the way it did. If things had turned out the way you planned, would there have been something else you might have missed out on instead? Perhaps you may have experienced other difficulties had it turned out the way you wanted.

By looking at things with less regret and more understanding you can connect with destiny and relieve some of the pressure of trying to plan your life perfectly.

AFFIRMATION: 'I am where I am supposed to be right now.'

EXERCISE: List at least one major thing you had planned for that never happened. Next to each one, write down one thing you would have missed out on, and one thing that might have been a struggle, if it had happened the way you planned it.

Underneath, write down something that happened instead that gave you joy that you might not have experienced had your initial plan succeeded.

Rejection ✦ Maturing

Rejection is something we all experience at certain times in our life and it's a difficult feeling to deal with. It can cause tremendous amounts of pain if we don't learn how to embrace it. When getting rejected it makes us feel inadequate, unwanted and perhaps like we are a failure. It can cause us to fear trying, feeling scared of moving forward and pursuing what we really want.

A common response is getting defensive and trying to stand up for ourselves, finding an excuse or even trying to hurt the ones that made us feel this way.

This is a vicious cycle that only creates more pain and hurt for both yourself and others.

This card challenges you to rise above yourself and your instinct to push away the rejection and instead stand higher knowing that rejection is not always a reflection of you as a person. Just because one thing didn't work out it doesn't mean that the whole of you is wrong. If you can raise your head and see above this, you can find peace in maturing and knowing that a rejection is only a push in a different direction for the time being.

Maturing can help you calm yourself down before reacting. Can you look the other way and break free from the cycle and find peace on the other side? Explore the rejections you've had and find, within them, what you are better off without. You don't need to prove others wrong; you don't need to prove yourself worthy or better, just know that you are enough and this rejection will lead you in another direction, and that is okay.

AFFIRMATION: 'I am confident enough to handle rejection. I do not fear rejection, it will lead me in a better direction.'

EXERCISE: Use the latest rejection that you experienced as an example. Journal on what happened, when it was, how it made you feel and what your response was then answer what has happened after.

- ♦ How would your life have been different had it not happened and how is it different now because it did?

- ♦ What are the great things you have experienced and now have because you got rejected?

This can make you see that rejections are not always a good or a bad thing, it just creates different outcomes.

Boundaries ✦ Respect

If you have pulled this card, you are being encouraged to take a close look at the boundaries you are setting and who in your life respects them and who doesn't.

Setting boundaries with people we love, and even people we don't particularly like, is not always easy. Sometimes you might not even know what your boundaries are straight away if being asked. Here's a chance to start analysing what your boundaries might be and where you would like to implement them more.

A big reason a lot of us are scared to set boundaries is the fear of rejection from other people. We're afraid that they will not respect it or they will say something mean or even stop being in our lives. But a question you might need to ask yourself is whether you really want those people in your life who don't respect you and your wishes. Might you be better off without them? If you let one person push your boundaries, they may get even harder to set in the future.

Even though you might have stated your boundaries to people, perhaps even multiple times, there are some that won't respect and honour them and will try to push them further and further back.

It might sometimes feel like you have to be clearer or reinforce the importance of the boundary you had set but please know that you don't have to get better at stating your boundaries, it is each person's own responsibility to be respectful to others and to you. Have a think about whether there is anyone in your life that is not honouring your boundaries and whether you need these people in your life.

In movies, respect is often presented as something you must earn. You need to prove yourself first to be worthy of respect. But is it true? If we look at it from our own perspective, do we really think that people need to prove to us first that they are worthy of respect before we treat them respectfully? Might it not be everyone's personal and individual responsibility to show respect for others? It is not your responsibility to make other people respect you, it is their responsibility to behave respectfully.

AFFIRMATION: 'I show my respect to others and equally deserve respect in return. I don't need to get better at stating my boundaries, I need to have people in my life that already respect them.'

EXERCISE: Next time someone says no to you accept it instead of trying to convince them, this way you are showing that you respect their boundaries.

And next time someone is trying to push your boundaries, make a mental note of it and consider whether this happens a lot with this person, and whether this person is actually good for you.

Apologising ✦ Grudge

It might feel easier to hold a grudge towards someone you had a fight with rather than take responsibility for and own your part in contributing to the disagreement.

You might have an inner battle of wanting to resolve the situation but hesitating to bring up the apology. There's often an internal push and pull; you want to resolve it but don't want to be the one taking the first step – it feels scary, humiliating, maybe even daunting.

Apologising is often seen as something weak, but isn't it really the ultimate strength? Apologising and taking responsibility for your actions is hard and therefore a sign of true strength – being willing to let go of your ego and trying to be better at showing the other person how strong you are and that you value your relationship more than this disagreement.

If you can find the strength to push away the feelings of resentment you can soften and make the relationship blossom again. Be courageous and own your mistake and you might find that the other person was feeling the same way, wanting to reach out to you but struggling to admit fault first.

We often think of apologising as giving up or surrendering and that apologising makes the other person right. But does it really? Saying I am sorry that I did this or said that is not saying what they did is okay. It only shows that you have good intentions and want to resolve the conflict. They might still be at fault even if you also were. A fight or a disagreement between two or more people is rarely only one person's fault.

This card wants to help you soften the grudges you might be holding and see your relationships flourish by helping you to find your own inner strength to admit fault.

AFFIRMATION: 'I am strong enough to admit my weakness.'

EXERCISE: Write an apology letter to someone that you have let down. You don't have to give them the letter or message yet, just use this as practice and perhaps with time it will feel easier to apologise when you do something wrong.

The letter needs to include what you want to apologise for, what you did wrong and ask for forgiveness.

Behaviour ✦ Interpretation

Behaviour is highly dependent on interpretation. We are intelligent beings and, therefore, how we behave is not simply a systemic reaction to what is happening around us. We have the ability to interpret, analyse and think before we take action. How we behave is a result of how we interpret the situation.

This card encourages you to keep an eye on your inner visions about other people's actions. What you tell yourself about what is happening and how you view the situation will affect how you react towards it.

Your actions aren't a result of other people's behaviour, but a result of how your mind interprets it.

It can be tempting to stay in your own mind and convince yourself that you are right, and more challenging to try and see something different to what you are telling yourself. But if you can start practising this you might find that your own mind can play tricks on you and what you see for yourself is not always the only thing there is to a situation. There can be multiple scenarios, explanations and resolutions.

The same goes for other people's actions. Have you ever sat and analysed in your head different scenarios of what people will do if you act in a certain way or say a certain thing? Most of us do this all the time about the tiniest things but their reactions are also a result of their own interpretation and doesn't have anything to do with you, what you say or what you do. There is no need to put all the blame on yourself either if something goes sideways. Other people have their own visions and interpretations that you cannot see or know so perhaps they also need to be forgiven for their behaviour sometimes.

AFFIRMATION: 'I don't simply react; I analyse and act.'

EXERCISE: Next time you feel a rush of anger, disappointment or get upset over someone's behaviour, note down two to three alternative explanations to their behaviour, except for the first thing you instinctively tell yourself. See if it changes how you feel about them.

True self ✦ Pseudo self

Life is a constant aim to find ourselves, be ourselves and show ourselves authentically to the world. But the reality is that we show many different versions of ourselves and not just one self. Sometimes we even show ourselves as someone we are not.

You might realise this about yourself too if you think about how you show up when you are with your family compared to with your friends, and again with your colleagues or strangers. You might see that how you act, what language you use, and what things you share or hide about yourself are different.

As you can see, there is not just one true self, one way to always be, there are different sides to us and we show different sides to different people. And that is okay. Showing your true self doesn't mean to show everyone all of us but to always show what is true, no matter which side of us it is.

Problems might occur for ourselves and others if we choose to show something else. This means not to make ourselves seem better than we are, but also not to pretend to be less than who we are. When we are challenged it's easy to slip into defensive mode and talk ourselves up to seem better than we are to prove our worthiness. Yet when our confidence is low we might instead put ourselves down and take more blame than we should.

This card challenges you to not make yourself seem either less or more when you are presented with uncomfortable truths and are being questioned or challenged.

Check in with yourself: are you in need of other people's validation to feel good about yourself? Are you depending on approval and praise from other people more than you are depending on yourself?

This might be a clue that you need to work on relying on and loving yourself instead of living in your pseudo self.

Remembering who you are is how you take your power back.

AFFIRMATION: 'I am who I am and I don't need to make myself look better or worse than what I am.'

EXERCISE: Next time you get the feeling that you want to show off, try and resist doing it if it isn't asked for. Also try and identify if you did something recently just for the sake of impressing someone and try to not do it again.

Forgiveness · Grimness

Forgiving someone doesn't make the thing they did to hurt you okay. Forgiving means setting yourself free of the pain someone has caused you. Forgiving someone is not for them, it's for you.

Not being able to forgive can cause grimness in your mind, negative and perhaps even intrusive thoughts. Holding on to the anger and other negative feelings will only inflict more pain on yourself.

This grimness doesn't necessarily even transfer to the very person or thing that you struggle to forgive, that you think negatively about and perhaps wish nasty things on. It mainly affects yourself, making you feel worse. It is like double punishment. You have already been hurt and now you are hurting yourself.

It might be hard to motivate yourself to find the feeling of forgiveness while still hanging on to negative thoughts, but forgiving someone is the best you can do for yourself. It might take some practice and repetition to truly let go, so be prepared and avoid judging yourself if you don't succeed immediately.

This card encourages you to try and wash away the grimness by forgiving in your mind. You don't have to tell the one who hurt you that you are forgiving them, remember it's not for them. You don't have to interact with them at all if you don't want to. See if you can let go in your mind and set yourself free from the pain that was caused.

It might help to reverse your perspective and see that the pain someone caused you merely means they have more growth to do, they couldn't do better and it's most likely a pain transferred to them from someone else that has been transferred to you. And now you have the opportunity to stop the cycle.

You are a beautiful individual and you deserve to flourish and move forward without grimness.

If you are blaming yourself, practice to forgive yourself as well and thank yourself for eventually getting out of the situation and doing the best you could.

AFFIRMATION: 'I set myself free by forgiving …'

EXERCISE: Whenever the grim thought about someone that hurt you comes up, practice repeating an affirmation and mantra that feels true for you in regard to the situation. For example:

'I forgive you, for you didn't know better.'

'I forgive you but it doesn't make what you did acceptable.'

'I forgive you for me.'

'I forgive and let go; I don't let this inflict more pain on me anymore.'

'I forgive you and wish you growth.'

Solution ✦ Problem

There can be many different solutions to the same problem, but even so it's easy to feel stuck in whatever situation you are in, feeling that you don't have any options at all, that you don't have the ability to change your situation or to solve the problem you are facing right now.

This card encourages you to think outside the box and be open to any solutions there might be to a situation at hand. Look outward to see what other people have done, but also look inward and see if you can feel the solution within you. Everyone is struggling with their own issues and nobody can solve your problems for you. Only you can be the one to do so.

Finding solutions can be difficult if you are in a situation of stress, your vision might be blocked and the only thing you can see and feel are the obstacles. You might feel like you are stuck between two mountains with nowhere to go. But mountains always have a base and there are ways around them, you don't need to do an impossible climb, you need to search for a different route and know that you are never stuck.

Sometimes the problem is not always finding the options either, you might find a lot of solutions but you are afraid of what might happen instead. Some situations call for brave actions, in some cases you might actually have to climb the scary mountain but find that what's on the other side was worth it. It might not be a big cliff edge to fall from, it might be a soft slope with a beautiful view and a sunrise welcoming you.

AFFIRMATION: 'I have the power and ability to change my situation.'

EXERCISE: Brainstorm ALL possible solutions with yourself no matter how crazy, scary or unrealistic they might feel. Write down every single solution you can think of on a small, separate piece of paper.

Pick one at a time and put them into two piles – the 'NO' pile and the 'MAYBE' pile. Narrow down the 'MAYBE' pile to the most feasible solution and you might find that you already had your answer within.

Energy ✦ Motivation

There are so many things in this world that easily drain both your energy and motivation to do things you might want to do. There are so many 'shoulds' being thrown around, both by others but also by yourself.

How often have you heard yourself say or think 'I should do this' and 'I should do that'? And not to mention the classic 'to-do list'. This feeling that we should but are not implies that what we currently are doing is not enough. This can lead to more stress and you might be even less likely to get things done.

The road to completing all the shoulds might seem endless and you can't see the reward that comes with it, only the pressure of doing better and doing more than what you are already doing.

By simply changing the language you use you will find it can reduce the stress related to certain things and hopefully restore the energy to do it and make you feel more motivated and positive towards whatever it is you think you should be doing.

What if instead of using 'should' you start using 'could'. 'I could do this' and 'I could do that'. It gives you an option; you can do it but you don't have to and it might reduce the sense of urgency and pressure.

This card encourages you to think about what language you use when you think to yourself, but also when you talk to others. See if there are any words you might want to change that can lead you to a more stress-free life, full of motivation and life energy!

AFFIRMATION: 'I *should* not do anything, but I *could* do anything I want.'

EXERCISE: If you have a to-do list, let's change it! Instead, make a must-not-do list or a could-do list.

21

Asking • Telling

Asking ✦ Telling

Asking questions and talking about our experiences are the fundamentals of conversations. They both have a place and they balance each other. If one or the other takes over, the conversation might lead down a narrow road especially when having a discussion, argument or misunderstanding with someone.

It might feel like there's a mountain between you if you focus only on getting your opinion or your side of the story through. If you show up to the conversation with an open mind to try and understand the other person's point of view, you might find that the mountain was really just a lake that you can swim across to reach the other person.

We often get stuck on focusing on our side of the story, trying to convince the other party that we are right or explaining to them how we feel. But if we show up to a conversation with the mindset of understanding rather than solving or explaining, we might get a different outcome – the resolution we were looking for in the first place.

This card encourages you to remember the balance in communicating and to think about how you have conversations with your loved ones, friends, family and colleagues or acquaintances. It encourages you to show up to the conversation with a different view in mind: to understand. Your goal is to be able to swim across the lake and not have you both stuck on opposite sides of a mountain, not able to reach each other.

Remember that conversations are not one-sided and it requires both parties to reach a resolution but you can be the one to start trying to move the conversation into a direction that focuses on understanding each other rather than telling each other. It might just help you both out.

AFFIRMATION: 'I show up to conversations to understand, not to prove I'm right.'

EXERCISE: Next time you have a conflict with someone, try and resolve it by avoiding pre-assumptions. In your head you might have made assumptions about the other person's opinion or point of view. This time, turn those assumptions into open-ended questions.

22

Sadness • Anger

Sadness ✦ Anger

Sadness and crying are often seen or portrayed as weakness, whereas anger is often portrayed as a powerful and strong emotion. No wonder it's much easier to express anger instead of sadness. But the expression of anger is often just a shield to the underlying emotion of hurt. Emotions that are seen as less valid, weak or even silly.

Anger is often used as a protective wall between you and other people. A shield to avoid showing your underlying vulnerability. If you ever see someone becoming angry about something, you can imagine there's a waterfall of tears hiding behind that expression.

This card encourages you to look behind the anger both in yourself and in others. When someone is getting angry and you can manage to change perspective and view it as sadness, you might feel that it becomes easier to help that person or resolve what they are actually angry about. It can help you to perhaps feel less defensive and help to resolve rather than escalate the situation at hand.

On the other hand, when you catch yourself harbouring feelings of anger and expressing those feelings, take a moment to stop and reflect and ask yourself whether you are really angry or is it something else that has made you feel hurt? Could you possibly address those feelings instead?

As anger and sadness are both powerful emotions you can be sure that whenever these feelings arise there is something in the situation that deserves attention as it is highly likely something that the person cares deeply about. Use this as a guide to find purpose and motivation both for yourself and others.

AFFIRMATION: 'I use my anger as a guide to my inner depth.'

EXERCISE: Learn to ask questions about the hurt rather than the expression of anger. When someone is expressing anger or you find yourself expressing anger, throw out the question: 'What are you/I feeling hurt about?'

Obliviousness ✦ Awareness

Uncertainty plays a big factor in triggering anxiety. It can be uncertainty about your living situation, whether a person likes you or not, whether someone might leave you, whether you'll get the job you applied for, whether your boss will like your work … the list can go on and on!

If you look at all these things and imagine a positive or a negative outcome, you might feel that the stress is not actually about the outcome itself but the fact that you don't know how things will turn out. Sure, you might not want the negative outcome of the two but you may prefer to know the answer for certain so you can act accordingly, rather than having to worry about which way it's going to turn out. You may also prefer to know that this person you are interested in doesn't like you in the same way, rather than having to guess and play detective to find out.

When you don't know a resolution to something it keeps your mind in a constant mode of analysing and weighing options and doesn't give you a chance to deal with the outcome yet.

Once something has been confirmed, there is a path of action and you can do something about it. If your boss doesn't like your work, you have the chance to improve, if you don't get a job you applied for, you can move on and look for something else. Not being able to do something can be more stressful than dealing with a negative outcome.

This card encourages you to come out of the unknown by taking action towards enlightenment in different situations. It might feel safer to hide below the surface rather than peeking up to see what's really going on but if you keep floating around in the bubble of the unknown it's highly likely that the anxious feeling you are harbouring won't go away.

AFFIRMATION: 'I am courageous enough to find out whatever answers I need to hear.'

EXERCISE: List three things that you keep ruminating about because you don't know the answer to. Write down the questions you need to ask, and to whom, to be able to find the answers. Collect your courage and send out the questions and be prepared to receive whatever answers you might receive.

Meditation ✦ Escapism

It's common to believe that the purpose of meditation is to think about nothing, empty your mind and get a rest from your thoughts, your inner dialog. But in reality, not to have any thoughts at all is nearly impossible as our brain is wired to do exactly that – think!

Meditation is not necessarily an escape from your reality, but a tool that can help you to see your true reality and reframe it and perhaps see it from a different light. It's a way to look at your thoughts from a more neutral perspective. It is thinking, but in a more structured way; instead of letting your thoughts roam free you try to slow down and analyse why these thoughts come up, what they really mean and whether they are true.

You might sometimes feel that you want to run away, be somewhere else and escape from your current reality. Common ways to do that is through watching tv, playing games, indulging in drugs or alcohol or anything that keeps your mind focused on one thing and makes you forget the things you don't want to deal with for a moment.

This card encourages you to lose yourself in your own mind instead of escaping into a different reality.

AFFIRMATION: 'I live and accept my own reality.'

EXERCISE: Next time you feel the urge to run away from your thoughts try and swap your go-to escape media for a guided meditation and see what happens. Guided meditations can be found in many different apps as well as online; do a quick search and see if you can find something that resonates with you.

Self-love ✦ Self-loathing

Self-loathing means putting yourself down and making yourself feel less than you are. It's the way you speak to yourself and the way you think about yourself. It is the opposite to self-love. Loving yourself doesn't mean you believe you are better than anybody else, but rather accepting you are not and believing that is okay. Nobody is better than anybody else, we are just good at different things.

If you pulled this card, it's an indication that you need to give yourself some love. Stop seeking it from others for a while and see what you can do to give it to yourself instead. It's time to look at yourself in the mirror and tell yourself lovely things rather than putting yourself down.

Take a moment and search your thoughts, especially the ones related to yourself. Look out for thoughts that start with 'I am …' and finish in something negative or start with 'I will never …' and end up with something you truly want. We all have thoughts like this and this card indicates that it's time for you to challenge those thoughts. Ask yourself if they are true or might there be a different side to them?

For example, if you tell yourself that you will never get your dream job, there is a high chance it is not a *fact*, rather just something you *feel*. What happens if you instead think: 'what is stopping me from getting my dream job?' or 'even if I might never get my dream job, I am still trying' or 'even if I don't get my dream job, I can be happy'. Perhaps change it to a question such as, 'what can I do today to get closer to getting my dream job?'

Self-love looks like 'I am not perfect, but I don't have to be' or 'I give myself permission to listen to what I need in this moment, rather than pressuring myself to do what I think I should be doing'. You don't need to punish yourself if you are not perfect, you don't need to force yourself to do things that don't feel right. You have the power to give yourself permission to accept that you are not perfect, and you don't have to be.

AFFIRMATION: 'I give myself permission to accept my imperfections.'

EXERCISE: Make a poster to help remind you every day to show yourself love and appreciation. Take your favourite affirmation or any words you feel inspire you to love yourself more. Here are some suggestions:

'I am not perfect and I don't have to be.'

'I love and accept myself for who I am.'

'I am enough; I am worthy.'

Fear ✦ Anxiety

Anxiety is often caused by fear or worry about something that has not yet happened. It might never happen or it might not happen the way you think it will. And the part of not knowing and fearing the worst can cause an anxious and very uneasy feeling.

On the contrary, after the event has happened, regardless of how it turned out, your anxiety will most likely ease if it was only tied to this specific event. So, the anxiety is not exactly related to the outcome, but the fact that the outcome is not known to us.

For example, you might feel anxious if you have a crush on someone and you worry that they might not like you back. But as soon as they either confirm or reject that they like you back, the anxious feeling is often gone. That doesn't mean you have to feel happy suddenly, but the anxious feeling might revert into something else.

Similarly, if you feel anxious about public speaking or doing a performance in front of people, you worry about how it will go, but afterwards there's often relief even if it didn't go as well as planned.

This card encourages you to reflect on the things in your life that might feel uncertain now. What are the things that you currently don't know how they will turn out?

Once you have acknowledged these things, see if there is anything you can do not to control the outcome, but to get clarity on the matter. Is there a way you can find certainty?

This might involve asking your crush how they feel about you, bringing up the problems you have with your friend or making a call and booking that health appointment you've been putting off because you are afraid of what the result might be.

As you can see, easing anxiety often means facing your fear, finding your courage and taking action. So, take that leap of faith and fly!

AFFIRMATION: 'I am afraid, but I will do it anyway.'

EXERCISE: In order to practice this, start with the smallest thing – whatever makes you least anxious of the things you have found. Analyse what it is you need to do to gain clarity. Take action, put it in your calendar (ideally as soon as possible) and afterwards cross it off your list and take notice of how your feelings have changed.

Offended ✦ Enlightened

Feeling offended by something is often a sign of an insecurity within yourself. The areas you have confidence in rarely make you feel offended if someone says something negative about it, because you know deep within yourself that they are wrong. It can cause a burning feeling in your stomach; you start to boil and arguments and things you'd like to defend yourself with pop into your mind. It can be truly exhausting so if you could learn to change your perspective you could save yourself a lot of energy.

This card encourages you to stop and think whenever these feelings come up. Ask yourself some helpful questions to be able to move on and not let it touch you. Ask yourself why you feel offended. Is the statement true to you or is it something that feels true at first glance, but maybe you will find it isn't if you take an extra moment to analyse it.

Noticing you are feeling offended can be used as a tool for yourself to find weak links that perhaps you need to work on. It can highlight the very areas that you haven't touched base with in a while but need to revisit and give some love and care to.

It can be helpful to pinpoint the topics that seem to cause you to feel offended. There's a high chance that these are things you like less about yourself, things that feel unfair or cruel in the world.

Instead of harbouring negative feelings, see if you can turn your perspective around and find enlightenment. See if you can find the reasoning behind the situation, an alternative explanation or even gratefulness.

Instead of letting the rage burn inside you, see if you can take a different road to enlightenment.

AFFIRMATION: 'I don't waste my energy on the road of rage, I stroll down the road of enlightenment.'

EXERCISE: Next time you feel offended, make a note of it and once you've calmed down from the situation ask yourself why you felt offended. Is the statement true about you? If it is, this is a sign that you need to work on loving that part of yourself too.

Freedom ✦ Sacrifice

Most of us like to think of ourselves as free. We have the right and ability to choose how we live our lives. But even so a lot of people feel stuck in the situation they are in and only dream about where they wish to end up. You might feel like you can't leave your job even if you aren't happy there, or that you can't move to a different place or look the way you wish or even travel as much as you want or to where you want.

This is because freedom doesn't always come for free. True freedom, rather than just being able to do anything you want, is being able to choose what to sacrifice in order to live the life you want.

If you can afford to sacrifice your job you are free to leave your current one. If you have time and energy to sacrifice to go and workout you could have the body you wish to have or if you are prepared to sacrifice your current security, you could perhaps travel anywhere you wanted.

This card encourages you to think about things in your life that, at the moment, you feel you cannot sacrifice in order to have the freedom you want. It is also to think about the things you wish for and see what sacrifices are necessary to make this happen.

What are the steps you need to take in order to gain the freedom you dream of?

AFFIRMATION: 'I am free to make my dreams a reality.'

EXERCISE: Make a 3x3 grid and in the first column list three things that you dream of doing but currently feel that you are not able to achieve.

In the second column, write down what it is that you have to sacrifice in order to achieve them.

In the third column, write down the steps you must take in order to be able to make those sacrifices.

Start from the third column and work your way back through the steps and you'll be getting closer and closer to your true freedom.

29

Cherishing • Suppressing

Cherishing ✦ Suppressing

Instead of trying to forget things, what if you allowed yourself to cherish the good parts of what was and perhaps even accept the bad things? Suppressing emotions and memories doesn't necessarily make them go away. The pain might go away temporarily, but every time the memory is triggered you will relive it even more intensely.

For example, after a breakup it is common to get rid of all the things that remind you of that person, but what if you could keep a few things that you used to cherish and reassign meaning to them? Instead of representing heartbreak, could it mean something new to you? Gratitude that you moved on. Happiness remembering the good times. Thankfulness for what it taught you.

This card encourages you to look at your memories with new eyes, not to be afraid of looking at the feelings that might come up for you around certain memories and seeing if you can see them in a different light to give them new, positive meanings.

It's time to stop hiding and trying to forget the things that have been only because they might have pain attached to them. It's time to open your eyes and see your memories for what they truly are and rewrite the meaning and purpose of them so you can move on with them and stop them from causing more pain.

Know that it is okay to miss what was once beautiful but no longer is. Things may have turned out for the best, but that doesn't mean it was all for nothing and not worth feeling and remembering the joy of it.

AFFIRMATION: 'I cherish the beautiful moments that have been and take the lesson with me of the things that caused me pain.'

EXERCISE: Find a belonging that you have kept that brings out mixed emotions for you. Perhaps a gift from a loved one that is no longer in your life.

Think about the memories it brings you, both the beautiful and the painful ones. See if you can neutralise the painful memories by giving them a different meaning.

For example, it might bring you pain because you are no longer with the person that gave you this gift, but because of how things turned out you might have learned something about yourself that can help you on your journey of love.

Appreciation ✦ Greed

Have you ever felt that you don't get enough verbal appreciation and positive feedback yet receive a lot of negative comments? It can feel lonely, like you're walking a long, hard road and dying for a drop of water to fill your empty cup of appreciation. In your search for that drop, you might miss out on an oasis had you changed your direction slightly.

It's easy to get stuck in a thinking pattern that focuses on what other people should be giving us and what we feel deserving of. Instead of lifting us up when we finally get it, the feeling of entitlement might take the edge off as we already thought we deserved it.

This card encourages you to search yourself and see if you can get the feelings of appreciation by giving to others what you are longing for. Ask yourself if you have shown appreciation to others. Have you taken the time to tell someone how much they mean to you and have you focused on giving positive feedback?

If you can turn your perspective around, you might find that it will bring you happiness and a feeling of importance and there's a high chance you will receive in return what you have unselfishly given without expecting it.

There might be a way to give what you've been missing to other people as well as yourself. Tell your loved ones what you would have liked to hear from them, such as 'you are beautiful', 'thank you for caring so much', 'I understand how you feel', 'I am sorry that I hurt you', 'you are right, I am sorry', 'thank you for always trying to understand me', 'you are always there for me, I really appreciate that' or 'you have the biggest heart'.

Make sure you tell yourself the same things you have been wanting to hear. Instead of waiting to receive it or looking for other people to affirm you, give generously to yourself.

Instead of focusing on what you want, what you deserve and what you should be given, focus on what you have to offer.

AFFIRMATION: 'I appreciate others and I appreciate myself.'

EXERCISE: Think about the things you don't feel appreciated for, either from your friends or partner or a family member. Write it down if you need to.

Now instead of focusing on receiving these things from them, take action and give to them what you are missing, and at the same time try and give it to yourself too.

Loneliness ✦ Connection

Feeling lonely isn't always caused by not having people around us, but by the lack of meaningful connections with the people in our lives. So even though you might have a lot of friends or you meet a lot of people on a daily basis, you can still feel alone.

Maybe the feeling arises when you realise there is no one to whom you can tell your inner secrets, nobody you can confess your pain to or nobody there that genuinely celebrates your success and happiness with you.

This card encourages you to look at the connections you have and see if there is anything you can do to improve them to make them deeper and more genuine.

Casual connections are easy to make but deeper connections are more meaningful and make us feel more fulfilled. So instead of fearing getting closer to others, see if you can lean in and nourish the relationships you have.

You have the ability to steer conversations in different directions. If someone is telling you about an experience they had, you can choose your questions and have them elaborate on how they were feeling in the moment, what they learned from that experience or what was the best versus worst part about it, or you can choose to focus on the more factual side of the story, such as where they were or where else they would like to go.

Start to be a bit more observant in your communication with others and see if you can notice opportunities for your connections to grow stronger and leave you both a little less lonely and a little more fulfilled.

Connection with others is daring to give of yourself, showing that it is safe to share with you and that you welcome their true emotions and listen without judgement.

AFFIRMATION: 'I fill my heart and soul with meaningful connections.'

EXERCISE: Choose the deeper questions in your conversations with the people you want to create a better connection with. Instead of focusing on surface questions and the facts of events, turn the focus onto their inner world. Ask about their thoughts and feelings and in the same manner, share yours with them.

Relaxation ✦ Activation

Not everything we think we know is true. And just because something cannot be proven, it doesn't mean it isn't there. If you are feeling uneasy, stressed or find it difficult to relax, know that it is not going to be there forever, things can change.

Just because it is there now, doesn't mean it always will be, it only means that there might be things in your life that you need to change. Have a think and write a list of things that currently make you feel anxious.

You are not your anxiety; it is just a feeling. But you are safe, you are not in danger and your body and mind together can make it go away.

Sometimes the best medicine for relaxation is activation. In order to be able to relax your mind, it can help that your body is also ready to do the same. Activating your body will help calm your mind and when your body is feeling tired you might also find it easier to relax mentally.

This card encourages you to try and find relaxation in your mind through activation of your body. Instead of stressing out your mind, see if you can shift your focus and let the stress out by moving your body.

AFFIRMATION: 'I let my emotional stress move through and out of my body.'

EXERCISE: Choose an activity that you enjoy, it may be as simple as going for a walk. While going through the motions, imagine your emotional pain or stress as fluid moving through your body with every move. If you are walking, visualise the feelings going through from where you can feel it, down to your legs and out through your feet. Or imagine your feelings as clouds evaporating from your body while moving through the exercises.

Action ✦ Reaction

Action and reaction might seem like similar concepts, but there is one significant difference between the two. A reaction is an instant almost impulsive response to something that is happening. An action, however, is a conscious decision made after consideration.

Reactions are mostly triggered by emotions whereas an action is determined after logical thinking. It's the thinking brain versus the emotional brain, and sometimes it can be difficult to distinguish the two.

This card encourages you to think about how you respond in different triggering situations. Are you in control of your response or are you not? If you find that you are not, it might be helpful to take time out when you feel triggered and use both your emotions and logic to find an appropriate response. Ask yourself if your initial thought is accurate and whether it is necessary for you to do anything at all.

Reacting can often cause regret as after we have cooled down from what triggered the response in the first place we can see the damage we might have caused. It is easier to see the situation in a different light when the trigger has stopped.

A helpful thing to do might be to try and find out what the root cause is of those triggers; can you find a pattern, are you always triggered in similar situations?

Also look back and see what things have helped you to be less reactive. Does it help you to go for a walk, visualise yourself in a different place, count to 10 or repeat a simple mantra?

AFFIRMATION: 'I act rather than react.'

EXERCISE: Find your triggers. Take a week or two and every evening before going to bed, write down things that triggered you during the day. You can identify those triggers either by the physical feeling in your body or through ways you have reacted that you might have some regret about later.

When you have a few things on your list, see if you can find a pattern there, for instance, is it always in relation to a certain topic, a certain person or perhaps a particular place?

Once you have pinpointed what your triggers are it can help you to choose action rather than reaction next time they happen.

Conflict ✦ Peace

Sometimes a conflict needs to escalate in order to reach peace. You might be holding something in to avoid confrontation, but the longer it boils inside of you, the harder it becomes to hold it in. Eventually it will escalate to a conflict either by action or by confrontation.

Like the beautiful sunshine after a heavy storm, the fresh smell in the air, the blossom and growth that comes as a result of the abundance of water, a conflict can also result in a beautiful outcome, personal growth and a fresh start. You might find that often after a conflict, the air has been cleared and peace is once again restored.

This card encourages you to think of conflict, or fear of conflict, as a sign that something is about to change and it is necessary that whatever is bothering you comes out in the open, in order to restore calm in your life.

You might want to try and see a potential conflict as a peacekeeping practice rather than just an uncomfortable interaction. In that way the conflict doesn't necessarily become as heated as you might have anticipated. If you go into a potential confrontation with an inner calm, you could feel that it's already on its way to a resolution.

Sometimes it is necessary to have an uncomfortable conversation or event in order to restore peace and create understanding.

AFFIRMATION: 'I face my conflict in order to restore peace.'

EXERCISE: When an issue is escalating for you, take action to resolve the conflict by opening the conversation with how you would like to create understanding regarding the issue. This way you can desensitise it and make it clear for everyone that there are good intentions and a call for peace and resolution, rather than conflict and fight.

35

Physical pain · Emotional pain

Physical pain ✦ Emotional pain

Your body and mind are highly connected and your nervous system runs through your whole body. If you have ever experienced a gut feeling, it is a very strong confirmation that your body knows what is going on emotionally or cognitively.

Emotional pain can manifest in your body and show up as physical pain. Especially if there is something troubling you that you have been ignoring for a long time. If you experience physical pain for no apparent reason, it's highly likely that it is stemming from emotional pain. It's a sign from your body to your mind to do something about what is bothering you.

This card alerts you to take note of any physical pain you might be experiencing and where emotional pain manifests for you. If you are experiencing difficult situations, try to be mindful of what it feels like in your body, whether it be pressure over your heart, a tight stomach or something else.

Stress is a common factor in causing physical pain so it is always good to be mindful and manage stress in your life. Staying calm even in stressful situations can help in aiding your body and managing pain. In the same way as emotions can cause physical sensations, you can use physical sensations to restore your mind.

AFFIRMATION: 'I am calm; I am grounded; I am safe.'

EXERCISE: Minimise stress by giving yourself some love, care and acceptance. Use the calming sensation of a hot bath and visualise and repeat in your mind: 'this water calms my body and mind'. Play some music that you like and imagine the sound waves vibrating your pain away or take a shower and imagine the water washing away the pain from your body.

Gratitude ✦ Indulgence

Gratitude is one of the best concepts to practice in order to live a happy and fulfilled life. It's easy to become lost in indulgence and try to acquire more and more – be it more things, more friends, more money or more fame.

When we are stuck in the indulgence mode, we often fail to see and appreciate what we already have. We may even have a lot of things that years ago we could only dream of, but we look ahead and strive forward instead of looking back and comparing with how life used to be.

This card highlights to you the importance of acknowledgement and appreciation of what you already have even though some days it might feel hard to find something to be grateful about. On your very worst days there are still things in your life that you can appreciate and perhaps even use to get through those terrible days. You might still have a safe home to go to or live in a beautiful location, have a nice dinner or a wonderful warm hug from a friend. Even small things such as the smell of fresh air when opening the window in the morning. If you think smaller and focus you can find so many things that are wonderful even on the darkest days.

AFFIRMATION: 'I feel grateful; I am grateful.'

EXERCISE: Start a daily gratitude journal. Get a new journal dedicated to this topic only. Write down at least one thing every day that you feel grateful for. Write as many as you can think of or if you are struggling write down one thing. Feel free to repeat what you were grateful for yesterday if it still feels true for you.

About the author and illustrator

✦

Hailing from Sweden and currently living in Sydney, Australia, Selena Moon has been interested in art, drawing and computers since childhood, and any free subject choices in school always tended towards the creative ones.

She has had her own design studio and years of experience with freelance design work that evolved to include illustrations and digital art. Selena now has an established and successful career as a graphic designer, illustrator and digital artist in both Sweden and Australia.

Her art is a mixture of digital collage, drawings and line art to create unique, bold, colourful and highly detailed imagery. She finds inspiration from various avenues and likes to explore new fields so she doesn't get bound by the same style or technique, utilising her many skills in combination to create unique pieces.

With an interest and study in psychology she combines her knowledge, own experiences and tools with her passion for art to create products that inspire and motivate people in their lives. What motivates her most to create art is the notion that it can help people, that the creations will have a purpose and potential to affect other people in a positive way.

Find out more at **selenamoon.co** or on Instagram: **@selena.moon.artist**